THE ALL NEW STYLE OF MAGAZINE-BOOKS

SDM

www.SDMLIVE.com

MP

MOCY PUBLISHING
WWW.MOCYPUBLISHING.COM

Printed by CreateSpace, An Amazon.com Company

In Memories of
Prince
June 7, 1958 - April 21, 2016

SDM

EDITOR-IN-CHIEF
D. "Casino" Bailey
casino@sdmlive.com

EDITORIAL DIRECTOR
Sheree Cranford
sheree@sdmlive.com

GRAPHIC/WEB DESIGNER
D. "Casino" Bailey
casino@sdmlive.com

A&R MANAGER
Aye Money
ayemoney@sdmlive.com

ACCOUNT EXECUTIVE
Frank Harvest Jr.
frank@sdmlive.com

PHOTOGRAPHERS
Treagen Colston
D. "Casino" Bailey

CONTRIBUTORS
April Smiley
Courtney Benjamin

COPY ORDERS & ADVERTISING OFFICE
Send Money Order or Check to:
Mocy Publishing
P.O. Box 35195
Detroit, Michigan 48235
(586) 646-8505
advertise@sdmlive.com

Copy Order Item #:
SDM Magazine Issue #7 2016
S&H Plus Retail Price - $9.99 per copy

WWW.SDMLIVE.COM

Printed by CreateSpace, An Amazon.com Company

MOCY PUBLISHING

CONTENTS

1

**ZAGG - InvisibleShield HD Glass Screen
Protector for Apple® iPhone®** $39.99
www.bestbuy.com

iPhone sold separately.

2

**Bose® - Solo 5 TV sound system -
Black** $249.99
www.bestbuy.com

3

**Kanto - YU5 5.25" 80W 2-Way Book-
shelf Speakers (Pair) - Gloss White**
$289.99
www.bestbuy.com

BARE ARMY

vs

EVERYBODY

SUNDAY APRIL 17

12900 Michigan Ave, Dearborn, MI 48126
CONNECTPAL.COM/BAREARMY

Streaming Music Is Now The #1 Source

IS STREAMING GOOD OR BAD FOR THE MUSIC INDUSTRY? WHEN DIGITAL DOWNLOAD SALES SEEM TO DROP, STREAMING MUSIC IS ON THE RISE.

by Cheraee C.

All the major music outlets including Apple, YouTube, Google, Tidal, and Spotify all offer streaming services to artists, mainly mainstream artists and the outlets have biased opinions about how streaming is truly affecting the music industry. Not only are the music stores offering better services, products, prices, features, and campaigns that outshine the other, but some outlets feel that streaming is hindering the music industry and other outlets are threatened by the revenue scale between a mainstream artist and an Indie artist.

SDM Live has recently joined the race of streaming while offering unlimited music streaming amongst other services and features unlike any other music streaming service. When an artists signs up on SDM Live website they get 80% of record sales of each single sold which is more then iTunes offers. SDM Live also has a music affiliate subscription program for artists to earn up to 25% revenue from customers who subscribe by using their affiliate link, which generates more revenue then the standard streaming service rate from any other streaming service. Music royalties are paid out weekly, and subscription affiliate royalties are paid out monthly. This gives the artist the ability to create music while getting paid on a weekly 9 to 5 basis.

Hot & Gritty New Book Release

PORSHA STERLING RELEASES HER NEW BOOK "KING OF THE STREETS, QUEEN OF HIS HEART" ON AMAZON.

by Cheraee C.

Porsha Sterling is an author at Leo Sullivan Presents: Sullivan Productions. Her hot, new book was just released May 1, 2016. The book kicks off with the main character Shanecia Jones returning home from college to find her mother dead from an drug overdose.

The mean streets of Miami is flooded with gangs and rivals. While Shanecia is on a spree to find the person responsible for her mother's tragic death, she ends up falling in love with a gang member, but no love in the streets comes easy.

Everyone questions their loyalty to their partner because their is constant tug of war between the heart and the mind. Add this book to your library especially if you love hood books and love stories.

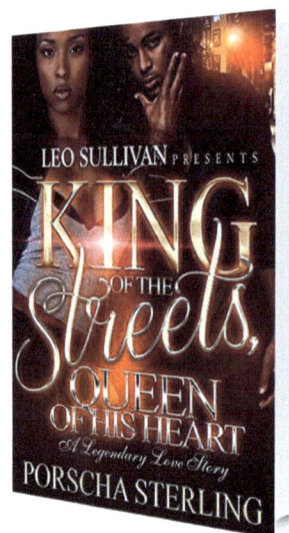

King of The Streets, Queen of His Heart
By Porsha Sterling

Available from Amazon.com and other online stores

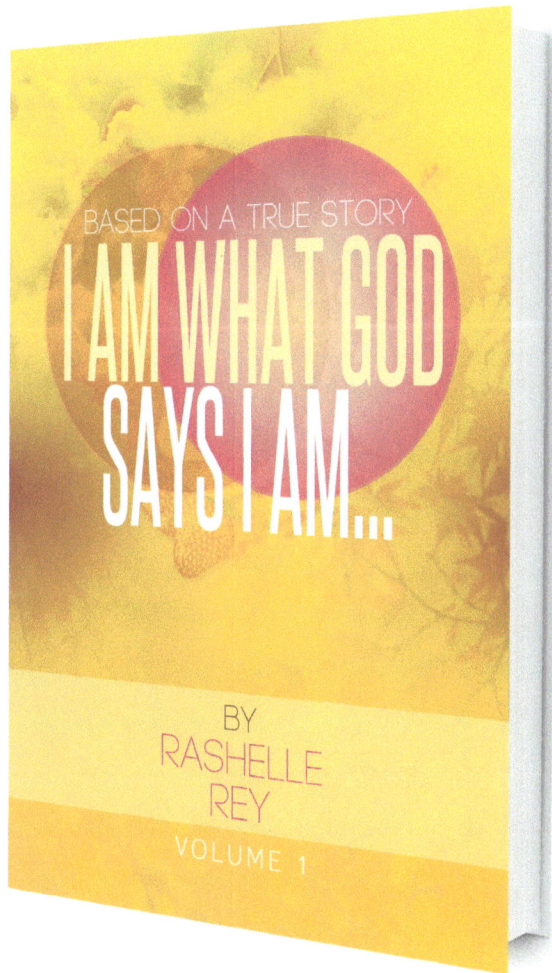

I AM MOTOWN

P-DOT: Respect The Hustle

DETROIT'S MOST RESPECTED FEMALE LYRICIST GETS PERSONAL ABOUT HER JOURNEY IN THE INDUSTRY, HER MUSIC, AND HER NEW DOCUMENTARY

by Cheraee C.

Q. How long has P-Dot been in the music business and what's your purpose as a female artist?

A. I have been rapping since the age of 14. I've been featured on various projects and collaboration albums with artists like Blackface, Big Herk, and J-Nutty of Rock Bottom, Malik and P-Frown of the East Side Cheddar Boyz and Live Action Entertainment. However, I wasn't serious about it. I decided to step out on faith two years ago and take this music business industry.

Q. How did it feel to perform and be honored at the Underground Hip Hop Awards?

A. It was both an honor and a privilege to be able to perform on one of the most respected stages in Michigan and that's Saint Andrews. To be honored, acknowledged, and accepted by icons like Carol Dorsey, Uncle P, Ikeisha Baker, and etc is affirmative that I'm moving in the right direction with my music and career. It was definitely an emotional experience for me. I didn't see it coming, but I always had faith.

Q. I know you got a lot going on in the music world and outside of it, so what's up with P-Dot and your documentary and your acting side?

A. Hip-Hop & Politics: The Documentary is a project being directed by director and photographer, Terris Walker. He contacted me to help bring awareness to my and surrounding communities. To stress the importance of voting because it's our only chance to have a voice. Now days, it's very few artists who support and give back. I want to make a difference anyway I can. I want to let our people, children, sons and daughters know, that we are important and we matter. That we are a threat; that when we come together we can make changes cause it's strength in numbers. I'm going to be in a couple of projects. "What People Do For Money," a novel turned movie written by Author Lasuria Allman, and a reality show spotlighting upcoming artists, black businesses, and etc titled "Hot In The Streets" Detroit Edition.

Q. Who is P-Dot behind the music, when its no stages, no beats, or no microphones?

A. P-Dot is just like anyone else. When I'm not working, I'm relaxing at my home or a family member's home, catching up or just doing absolutely nothing. Lol, I like to read and get caught up on my favorite reality shows lol.

Victory Entertainment Group

A HOT, NEW DETROIT LABEL RISING UP FROM POVERTY AND INTO SUCCESS WITH ITS INTEGRATION OF MODELS, ARTISTS, AND IT'S VICTORIOUS VISION.

by Cheraee C.

Q. Okay J. Hustle, who is the creator of the movement Victory Entertainment and why did you choose that name to represent your business?

A. Myself and Jay Lavon created Victory Entertainment group in a one bedroom apt. We had nothing to our name, just a love for music. Jay lived with his mother in the apt and supported the household as she was having a hard time finding work. I had to move back with my pops; I had a DUI, and I had lost my job, and had nothing to my name. Victory was a vision of something we wanted. It was us striving and working hard giving our all to overcome poverty and to change our environment for the better. Victory is for anyone that has faced a challenge and overcame it. This is more than a record label in our life.

Q. Who are all he members of Victory Entertainment and what are all their strengths? Does everyone rap, sing, or both or have other talents?

A. The artists are J. Hustle (myself), King Tut, Chris Khronic, RG Baby, Tone, and Two Face Sauce are the rap artists. We just attained an r&b artist who is Kenyatta Rashon.

Q. Would you say Victory Entertainment is a movement, or a lifestyle, and what's the next event you guys have?

A. It's definitely a movement. For a long time our city Ypsilanti has had a hard time supporting each other due to selfishness, but we are out to break this chain and support any artist that is working to make it in this industry. We have a firm belief in investing in yourself and helping each other achieve their goals. The next event we have is 6/11/16. We have teamed up with Self-Employed Records and Infynite Promotions to bring Mia X and Mystikal out to the Detroit West Club where J. Hustle (myself) will also be performing.

Q. What city are y'all from?

A. Ypsi, Y-town, Ypsilanti. I call it Ypsilanta because of all the talent that is here. We are soon to be the new mecca of music.

Alicia Brings Amity To Children's Books

MRS. WHITE IS SPREADING HER GREATEST MESSAGES TO THE YOUTH THROUGH HER SERIES OF EDUCATIONAL CHILDREN'S BOOKS

by Cheraee C.

Q. Out of all the literary genres there are, what made you want to write children's books?

A: Well, actually, the answer to this question is two-fold... First, as a mother and professional educator, I've always been charged with guiding and encouraging young children to seek progress on a social level. So the role of communicating to them in this manner just comes naturally, to me. Second, with the modern ways of society influencing our children, I feel like it's necessary that we as adults, take full responsibility for enlightening our babies. It was my desire, along with co-author Victor Walker, my fiance, to establish an outlet where we could inform, Educate, and inspire them-all through one medium. And so, writing children's books was the end result.

Q. What is the main message that you are portraying in your collection of children's books, or are there multiple messages being portrayed?

A. Yes, there are multiple messages being portrayed in our collection of children's books... In our first series, "The Moral Adventures of King Ray-Ray," the message is, you can do anything that you set your mind to do, as long as you believe in yourself! Our second series, "BEWARE OF MR. NO-NO!!!," teaches children the importance of not interacting with strangers, and to always be aware of their personal surroundings. In our most recent series, "What Would Lil' Jesus Do?," the message is based upon spiritual enlightenment and the basic rules of living righteously as a child of God. We also have many more children's books scheduled for release, and they each bear very important messages.

Q. When you're not writing children's books, what do you do in your spare time?

A. At this point in my life, I really don't have any spare time. However, when I'm not writing children's books, I'm both a full-time mother and a budding entrepreneur. I'm also deeply involved in many church functions and community events. Recently, I launched my first line of Inspirational/Christian merchandise @ www.facebook.com/1 OAK Inspirational/Christian Merchandise & Accessories, By Alicia B. I also have a new designer handbag collection called, "Christian Couture." Ultimately, my main goal in life is to be happy, healthy, and successful, so most of my time is geared towards 'building' to those ends. I love my life and I have plans to live it to the fullest!

Jennings Got The Motor City Smoke

NEP IS A VISUAL HIP HOP INNOVATOR WHO UTILIZES ALL THE DIGITAL AND MECHANICAL ASPECTS OF MUSIC TO THE FULLEST.

by Cheraee C.

Q. Who is Nep Jennings as an artist inside the booth and outside the booth?

A. I am an original hip-hop writer, videographer, performer, artist, producer, and music engineer from the city known as the murder mitten. When I'm out the booth, I spend my time with my family and loved ones. That's where my inspiration comes from to create.

Q. I know that you and JP One collaborated on the album Real Motown Music together, so how do you feel about the album overall and what's your favorite track on the album and why?

A. A few of my personal favorite tracks on the album first is "Nothin" which is one of the earlier tracks recorded on the album. I personally enjoy it so much because it relates to a real life situation that I went through, and it really set the tone to keep the bar up for the rest of the material on the album. My second favorite is "World Going Crazy," another track produced by Flamin Lacez. This song is a little different than the average material of the hip-hop genre because me and JP One touch on a few sensitive and controversial subjects not being scared to speak your mind and the conditions of the world, and being raised in the ghetto.

Q. Who was the most memorable artist that you've worked with so far and why whether it be on a track, videography, or musical engineering?

A. My most memorable person that I have worked with so far personally would be Flamin Lacez the producer. He brings a different and more aggressive side out of me when creating.

Q. Since you've been in the industry, how have the people around you changed from new friends, to old friends, or ended friendships?

A. Not much has changed since I've been working in the music industry with my family and friends. I still rock with the same people I've been with since day 1. The people that changed are not close to me so it really didn't affect me that much in a negative way. I use all energy for motivation.

SDMLive.com is now Streaming Live High Quality Music. Listen to all new Exclusive Music Unlimited for $7.99/mo. Subscribe today!!!

GET UNLIMITED EXCLUSIVE MUSIC ANYTIME...ANYDAY!!!

www.SDMLive.com

The Prince Scandal

PRINCE ROGERS NELSON SUDDEN DEATH IS RAISING EYEBROWS ALL ACROSS THE WORLD.

by Semaja Turner

Conspiracies are flying left and right like airplanes about another sudden death in the music industry from the iconic legend Prince. Some theorists are alleging foul play saying he had AIDS, he was drugged, or his death was the result of a music mafia group who kills or shames anyone that doesn't surrender to them and their demands. Prince's death is such a scandal that his autopsy report will never reveal to the world how he really died in an elevator in his home. Whatever the cause of death really was, the world is still mourning from the loss of a very opinionated and diversified legend.

Theatres, radio stations, music artists, and magazines all over the world have been paying all types of tributes to Prince in memory of him and his huge impact to the music industry. Before his death, he was speaking the truth a lot about his past, record labels, the hypocrisy in politics, being a Jehovah Witness, and many other issues. Prince was on to something new in his world of creativity and wasn't afraid to expose or impose anyone or anything.

Now that a healthy and wealthy man has been silenced by death, hopefully the truth will continue to manifest, and Prince's death will not end as a mystery or a scandal.

Esko: Detroit's Black Jesus

THE EASTSIDE RAPPER WHO GREW UP ON LENOX AVE IS DETERMINED TO MAKE A NAME FOR HIMSELF AND CONQUER DESPITE OF HIS OBSTACLES.

by Cheraee C.

Q. What's been going on with you since your last interview in the 2nd issue of SDM?

A. I been finishing up the "Mudwave" White Line Feva project. I just recently released the video 5/01/16.

Q. On social media, you call yourself Jesus Esko. Why did you give yourself that name?

A. It's only Esko; it stands for eastside K.O.. Jesus Esko is just a Facebook name because I look like the man they describe as to be Jesus in the Bible. E.S.K.O is just an acronym for East Side K.O., of course you know what K.O. mean. It ain't no da vinci code or nothing lol, but the real definition is documented in audio on this project.

Q. What's going on with your single "Mean Something", and the person who produced that track?

A. Something happened with his YouTube video about copyright issues and he said I had something to do with it, but I don't know what happen... I told him I'll pay for any damages, but shit I might not lol. The shit happened twice lol. I don't know how it happened by it's all on my YouTube comments.

Q. So did you and the producer work things out or is it still a situation?

A. The producer was pissed saying it was a copyright claim on the my song and that I didn't give him or his proper or credits for the beat and that he was done giving away free non-profit beats. Some comments were disabled, but I think he could've handled it a lil differently or it couldn't have been me.

Q. It seems like your an underrated artist, but definitely not in SDM's eyes. Why do you think people don't support you?

A. Once you understand me then you'll be able to listen through this project and feel me and be able to understand who I am and why I'm talking the way I talk. Yo baby got hit records all on the tape and everything a buck from the shot all the way down to the tape 100.

Q. Coming from where you been, how does it feel to be on the cover of this month's SDM Magazine?

A. This shit big, yo baby ain't dropped nothing or even talked to the public in a minute and to be able to be here soon as I was finishing up my project. This is a blessing for yo baby.

Q. What made you get dreads, and do you feel like your dreads add to your passion of music?

A. Lol I got dreads cuz I was tired of braid, but when you make a certain choice to do shit, then you start to understand the difference it make to your everyday life. You learn yourself a lil more so I'd say yes. For instance, I don't watch TV or play video games and that's usually what they talk about in barber shops so I can avoid hearing what I don't care for at certain times you following yo baby? I can just sit between a bitch legs at the crib n get twisted n figure out how I'm a be the conversation in the barber shop.

Q. It's a lot of artists on the eastside including yourself. How do you feel about these artists on the eastside and their music?

A. Well, I can't really speak on them in a negative way because whether I like it or not, it's something they putting their effort and money into and I can't do shit, but respect it you feel me? What separates their music from mines is we different people with different ways of communication and ideas.

Q. I know you always working so when do you find time to do music and what do you do in your spare time?

A. I ain't got no spare time...I'm always moving...climbing mountains, jumping over planes you feel me? I got three kids in three different cities so I can't stay still. I create the music throughout the day. I ain't got no sit down time to write. Shit honestly, I'm creating while we doing this interview. You can kind of get that feel on the song "Go."

TOP 10 CHARTS

TOP 10 DIGITAL SINGLES AND ALBUMS
MAY 1, 2016

TOP 10 CHARTS

DRAKE BREAKS A NEW RECORD WITH OVER 20 SONG ON THE TOP 100 BILLBOARDCHART.

TOP 10 SINGLES CHART OF THE MONTH

No.	Artist - Song Title
1	DRAKE - ONE DANCE
2	BEYONCE - LEMONADE
3	DEJA LOAF - ALL JOKES ASIDE
4	J COLE - NO ROLE MODELZ
5	DESIIGNER - PANDA
6	RIHANNA - WORK
7	KING DILLON - WILT
8	DRAKE - SUMMER SIXTEEN
9	ESKO - WHITE LINE FEVA
10	CHRIS BROWN - LIQUOR

TOP 10 ALBUMS CHART OF THE MONTH

No.	Artist - Album Title
1	BRYSON TILLER - TRAPSOUL
2	TWEET - CHARLENE
3	DAVID BANNER - BEFORE THE BOX
4	KEVIN GATES - ISLAH
5	FUTURE - EVOL
6	KANYE WEST - THE LIFE OF PABLO
7	TYRESE - BLACK ROSE
8	TANK - SEX, LOVE & PAIN II
9	J. COLE - 2014 FOREST HILLS DRIVE
10	KOSTA - D.I.Y.

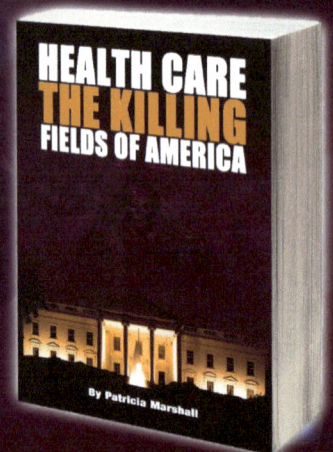

ALBUM REVIEW

TOP 3 ALBUMS THIS MONTH

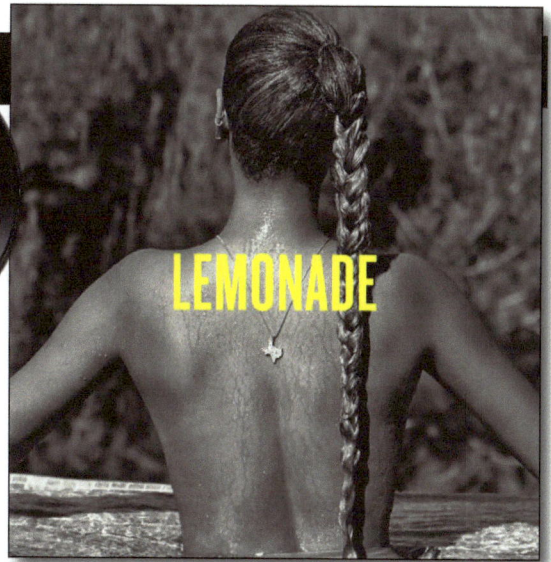

LEMONADE

Lemonade

ARTIST: Beyonce
REVIEWER: Cheraee C.
RATING: 3

Queen Bey just dropped some major lemonade on the music industry with her brand new visual album she released on HBO first. She has her viewer ratings on a million as she gives us melody, eye candy, and attitude for days. The queen of creativity is always changing the game with the way she releases her music. Her tracklist includes tracks from Sorry, Don't Hurt Yourself, 6 Inch ft The Weeknd, Forward featuring James Blake, Freedom featuring Kendrick Lamar, Sandcastles, Don't Hurt Yourself featuring Jack White, and more. I give this album three stars.

RATE METER: 1 - WACK   2 - NEEDS WORK   3 - STRAIGHT   4 - BANGER   5 - CLASSIC

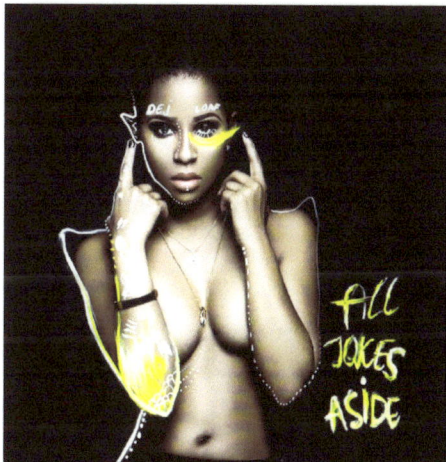

All Jokes Aside

ARTIST: Dej Loaf
REVIEWER: Cheraee C.
RATING: 4

These days Dej Loaf is definitely coming out her shell and showing us more of her feminine side as she puts all the jokes aside with her new mixtape. Her tracklist includes Vibes, Who Am I, Chase Mine, Goals, Money on the Flo, Givin N Takin, Chase Mine, and many more. I give this mixtape four stars.

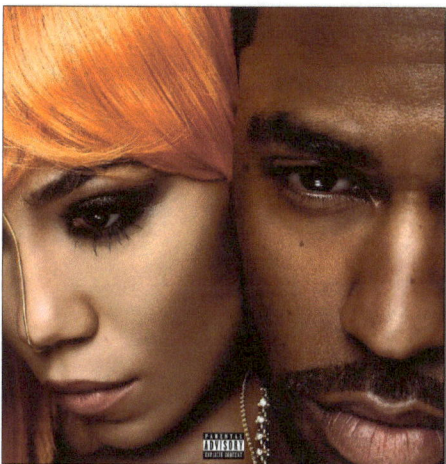

Twenty88

ARTIST: Big Sean/Jhene Aiko
REVIEWER: Cheraee C.
RATING: 4

Detroit's own Big Sean and singer Jhene Aiko team up for a very enticing 8-track collab album with a smooth blend of rapping and singing. Some of the hottest tracks from the album include London Bridge, Memories Faded, Selfish, De Ja Vu, On the Way, and Push it. I give the album four stars.

Celia

is a popular model from Detroit, MI. that loves fashion.

facebook

I Model
Celia Harris

HEELS &
SKILLZ

Photography by
@barearmy

HEELS &
SKILLZ

Cache

is a beautiful model
from Las Vegas, NV.
make up by
@georgemckinney

instagram
@therealladycache

Photography by
@barearmy

HEELS & SKILLZ

Precious Houston

Work in medical field, in school for cosmetology, have own marketing company and from Ann Arbor, MI. 27 years old

instagram
@Fleetmodelprecious

Photography by
@Doug Sims

Cheraee's Corner

WHY DO WOMEN THINK THAT MEN ARE SUPPOSED TO DO EVERYTHING IN A RELATIONSHIP WITHOUT SUPPORT?

by Cheraee C.

I was watching a web series titled "Life Goes On" from Detroit. I was highly agitated on the third episode when a character said, "her household was struggling, her and husband lost their jobs, there was no income in her home, and she didn't want to work because she felt like her husband is the head of the household and she shouldn't have to work. That's a very lazy and stupid mentality consuming a lot of women. What kind of woman doesn't want her own money? What kind of woman feels like she's incapable of working? Only women who are entrepreneurs and self-employed are women who don't have to have a 9 to 5. Other then that every woman should have a working and legit hustling attitude whether married or single. Every woman should be focused on being financially stable whether married or single, whether childless or with children.

Women really need to stop making other women look bad by entering relationships for the wrong reasons. Don't use a relationship to come-up in life because there will always be a downfall when it comes to pure selfishness. Life is what you make it, so when you enter a relationship, remember to remain truthful.

NEXT 2 BLOW

KENYATTA RASHON

Q. How did you manage to become apart of the Queens of Diamond showcase?

A. I have done some work with Mobdiva and she actually put all of this together. I have been working really hard on the scene and behind the scene. When she asked me, I was absolutely interested!

Q. How have you been grinding on the scene and behind the scene in general as an artist trying to succeed in the industry?

A. On the scene, I'm trying to gain as much exposure as possible. Doing shows from 734 to 313; even when I perform I love to do a snippet of a cover to engage the crowd before I perform my original. Behind the scenes, when I'm not working on my individual artistry, I'm making people feel good as the lead singer in the "Emerging Soul" Band out of the Metro Detroit area. Behind the scenes, I've been doing a lot of research so once my hard work pays off, I can swim instead of sink. Also, I've been collaborating with different local artists and producers to make sure I can release quality work.

Q. I know people in the industry have multiple talents so what other talents do you have besides being an artist?

A. Well, coming up as a kid, I made sure I was a triple threat (acting, singing, and dancing.) I've starred in school plays and musicals. I loved acting, but its gotten away from me since I've become the artist I am today. But I still get a chance to utilize one of my other talents including professional arguing as well as an unlicensed psychologist which is one of my favorite subjects.

Q. Your artist name is very different. How did your name come about and how long you been pushing your music.

A. The name Sounds just came to me one day and it stuck with me. I changed my name a few times in the past, but Sounds was the only thing that felt right. It was almost as if the name came to me by divine intervention because as soon as I said it, the first time I just knew. Kinda like Clairvoyance. I often close my eyes and see huge stage lights with the letters spelling Sounds flashing. I close my eyes and I see huge masses of people cheering. I see myself standing center stage happy and excited.. Feeling alive .. yea Sounds lol. I've been creating music pretty much all my life, but as far as really taking everything serious, I've been doing music professionally for the past eight years.

Q. Out of the eight years in this industry, what is the hardest obstacle that you've had during this journey and how did you overcome it?

A. That's a tough question. I'd say the hardest obstacle I had to face and conquered would be finding myself as an artist. As I said before wit all my name changes... I had to become comfortable with myself. I had to learn how to express myself freely without worrrying about what other people would think or say. So long as my actions didn't harm anyone else both mentally and physically.. I had to learn how to be confident in myself in my abilities.. So conquering myself would be the best answer to that question.

Q. Is music a passion, a hobby, or a sport to you and what are you currently working on?

A. Music is not only my passion, but my life. I don't know how anyone could ever live without music... being able to create such great music is a gift I am truly thankful for and because I am truly grateful for my gift to create such spledor music... my plan is to help as many people as I can whether it be by the words of the songs that I write or by the blessings that I receive from the music that I create. After all I am a philanthropist. Currently, I am working on a solo project entitled "Angels in The Outfield" and honestly that's pretty

Sounds

much done and ready to be released June 20th this year. The album is quite magnificient if you ask me. I even got some production from Super Producer Helluva thrown in there and a feature from the extremely talented and gorgeous Neisha Neshae. So I'm really excited and looking forward to the release of that project.

Juan TheDon

Q. Who is Juan Thedon and how long have you been in the industry?

A. Well, I've been rapping for 14 years, but I only been serious the last three years about the craft.

Q. Why did it take it over 10 years for you to get serious about rapping?

A. Well, I'm 27 now. I always rapped with friends in my neighborhood. It was not until I became an adult that I got more serious and started actually recording music and doing shows. I always wanted to do music since I was a little guy. I was fascinated with classic rock and roll. When I was a kid, music was always a big part of my childhood . I was 10 years old when I first heard Eminem for the first time and I fell in love with hip hop.

Q. What other crafts do you have and what do you do when your not rapping?

A. Well, I like to write a lot. I write verses and hooks for upcoming songs. I'm always writing. Music is my life. I don't have any other hobbies and there's not anything else I like to spend my time doing.

Q. Out of these three years of taking your music seriously, what is the best song that you made and why?

A. I think it's "StunnaBoi" and it's my best song cause everyone loves it live.

SNAP SHOTS

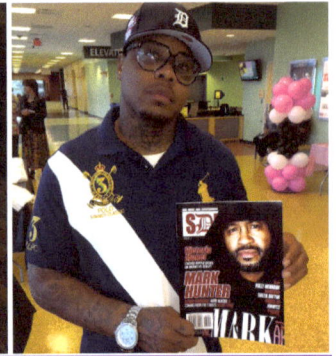

Email Your Snap Shots to
snapshots@sdmlive.com

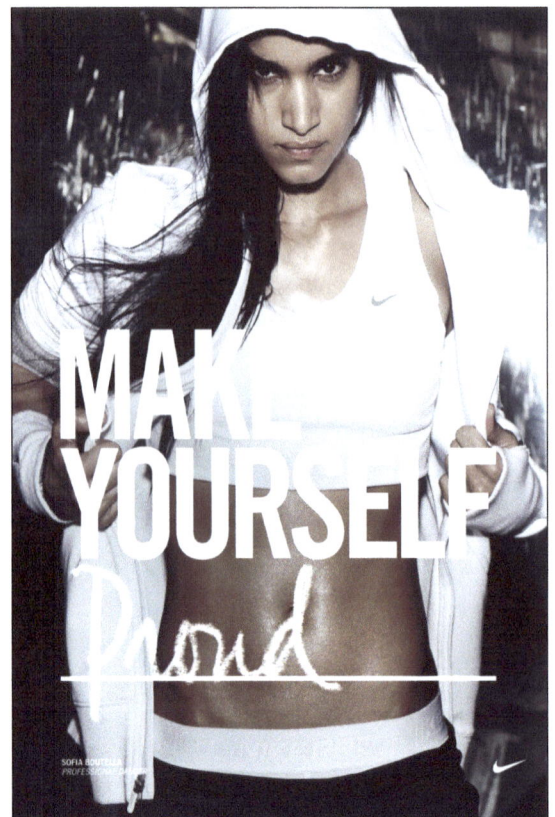

MAKE
YOURSELF
Proud

SOFIA BOUTELLA
PROFESSIONAL

REAL MUSIC. REAL ENTERTAINMENT.

S.D.M

ISSUE 3

KOSTA
JUST HIT THE JACKPOT WITH A NEW SMASH HIT SINGLE "LOTTERY"

BIGG DAWG BLAST
LAUNCHES THE STREET HITTA DJ'S MOVEMENT

Neisha Neshae

BRINGING IN 2016 ON STAGE WITH THE KING OF R&B R-KELLY & DROPPING A NEW MIXTAPE

PLUS MORE

THE RED CARPET EDITION
SUPERSTARS CAME WITH FASHION AT THE SDM MAGAZINE RELEASE PARTY

US - $9.99 CANADA - $14.99

01 >

9 770317 847001

JANUARY 2016 No.3
WWW.SDMLIVE.COM

Urban Fiction, Spiritual, Motivation and more.
Order a book from Mocy Publishing today and receive FREE shipping.

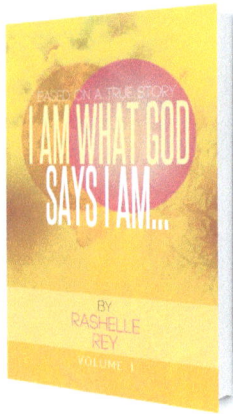

I Am What God Says I Am...
By Rashelle Rey

Item #: IAWGS29
Price: $9.99

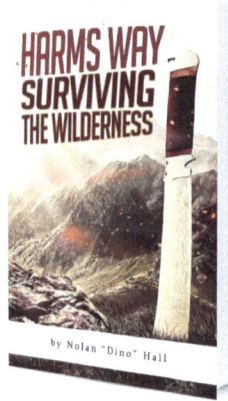

Harm's Way
By Nolan "Dino" Hall

Item #: HWS821
Price: $15.99

The Shadiest Mission Ever
By Cheraee C.

Item #: TSME28
Price: $12.99

The Son Of Scarface – Part 1
By Stanley L. Battle

Item #: TSOS01
Price: $12.99

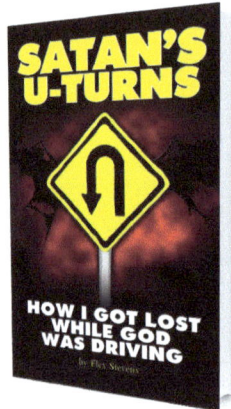

Satan's U-Turns
By Flex Stevens

Item #: SUT382
Price: $9.99

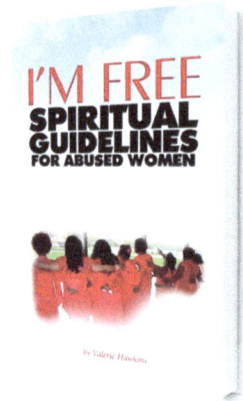

I'm Free
By Valerie Hawkins

Item #: IFTSG82
Price: $14.99

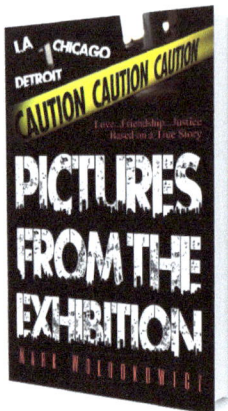

Pictures From The Exhibition
By Mark Wolodkowicz

Item #: PFAE292
Price: $15.99

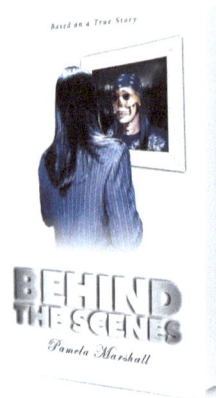

Behind The Scenes
By Pamela Marshall

Item #: BTS721
Price: $15.99

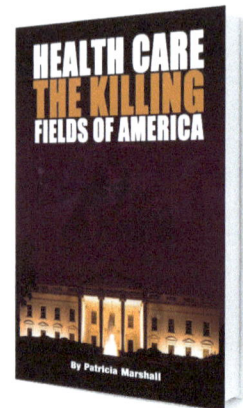

Health Care
By Patricia Marshall

Item #: HCTABF2
Price: $17.99

www.mocypublishing.com
order online and receive FREE shipping. Limit time offer.

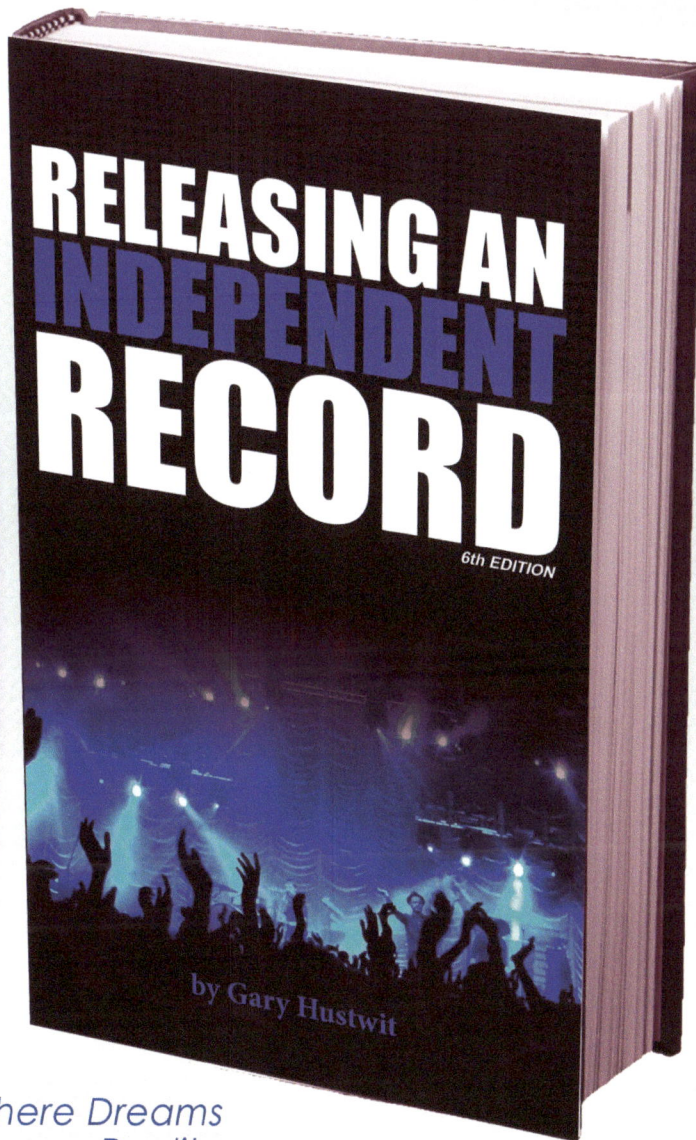

THE ALL NEW STYLE OF MAGAZINE-BOOKS